Identifying Chincoteague Ponies

The print alternative to the *Chincoteague Pony Names* smart phone app.

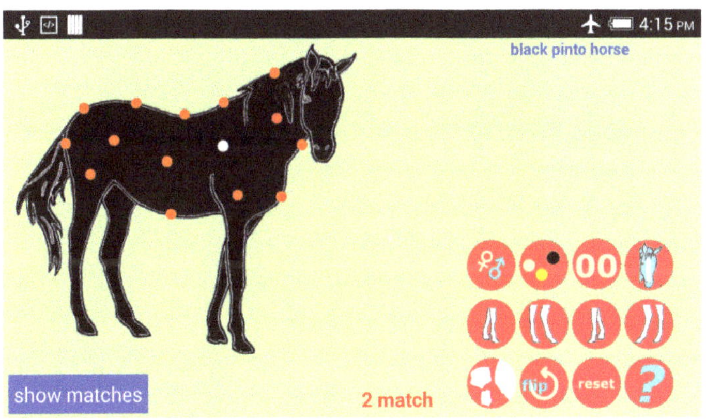

Fall 2017 Edition

Other books from
Jennie's Music Room Books

Nicio and Cedar Fire
Legends of Two-Legs

Jennie's Music Room Books
4241 Filmore St
Chincoteague Island, VA 23336

ISBN: 978-0-9842392-5-2

Library of Congress Control Number: 2017944483

Contents

Ponies

Bay 2
Bay Pinto 28
Black 94
Black Pinto 96
Buckskin 112
Buckskin Pinto 128
Chestnut 138
Chestnut Pinto 180
Palomino 242
Palomino Pinto 250
Silver Dilute 262
2017 Buy Backs 270

Indices

Alphabetical 273
Stallion 282
Brand 283
Other Resources 288

Color Definitions

bay: Any dark colored horse with black points*. Colors range from shades of red to very dark brown.

black: An all black horse including points*.

buckskin: Any light colored horse with black/brown points*. Colors range from very light cream to yellow, tan, or gold.

chestnut: A reddish brown horse. Colors range from light red to deep mahogany.

palomino: A pale horse with white mane and tail. Colors range from cream to golden.

silver dilute: A bay or black horse with a 'silver' gene that results in a blond mane and tail, 4 socks/stockings and a lightening of the coat.

**points*: legs, muzzle, mane and tail, and tips of ears

Bay

Bay Girl

Fluffy
mare
brand: none

Bay Girl

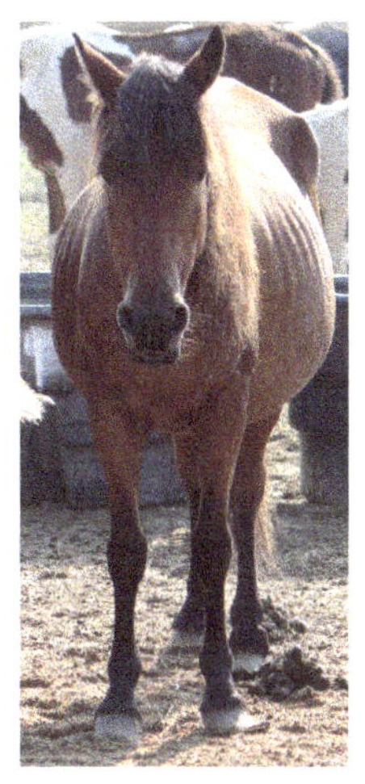

Bay

Daisey

mare
brand: none

Bay

Daisey

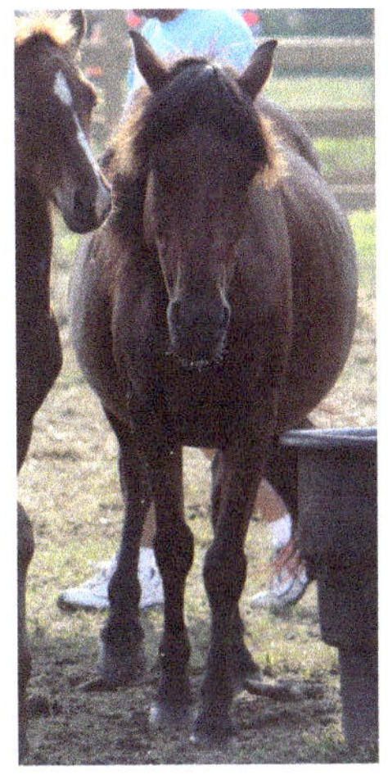

Bay

Effie's Papa Bear

Poseidon's Fury, Hoppy
stallion
brand: unreadable

Effie's Papa Bear

Bay

Galadriel

mare
brand: none

Galadriel

Bay

Little Dolphin

Neptune
stallion
brand: 08

Bay

Little Dolphin

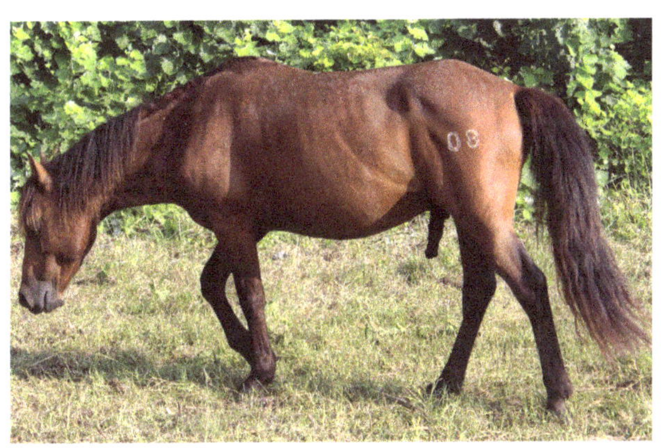

Bay

Pappy's Pony

mare
brand: 03

Bay

Pappy's Pony

Bay

Pony Ladies' Sweet Surprise

Lady
mare
brand: 04

Pony Ladies' Sweet Surprise

Bay

Two Teagues Taco

Taco
mare
brand: 05

Two Teagues Taco

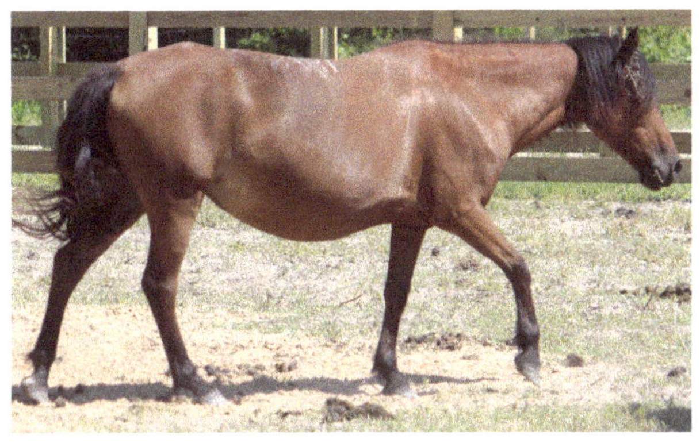

Bay

Unci

mare
brand: none

Bay

Unci

Bay

Jean Bonde's Bayside Angel

Angel
mare
brand: 15

Jean Bonde's Bayside Angel

Bay

Leah's Bayside Angel

mare
brand: unreadable

Leah's Bayside Angel

Bay

Dakota Sky's Cody Two Socks

Cody
mare
brand: 05, partial

Bay

Dakota Sky's Cody Two Socks

Bay

Bling Bling

Diamond's Bay Dream
mare
brand: 15

Bling Bling

Bay Pinto

Rosie's Teapot

mare
brand: 13

Rosie's Teapot

Bay Pinto

Summer Breeze

Cee Cee, Breezy
mare
brand: none

Bay Pinto

Summer Breeze

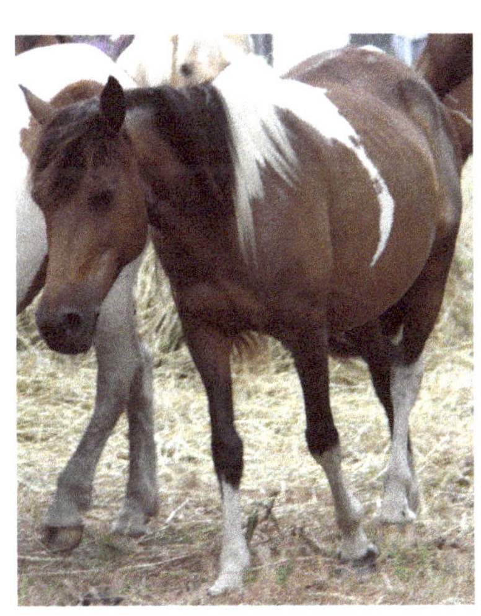

Bay Pinto

Ella of Assateague

Ella
mare
brand: 00

Ella of Assateague

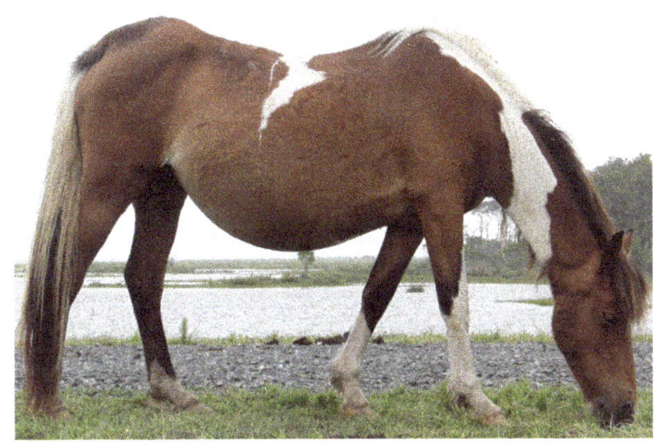

Bay Pinto

Cody's Little Jigsaw Puzzle

Jigsaw
mare
brand: 13

Bay Pinto

Cody's Little Jigsaw Puzzle

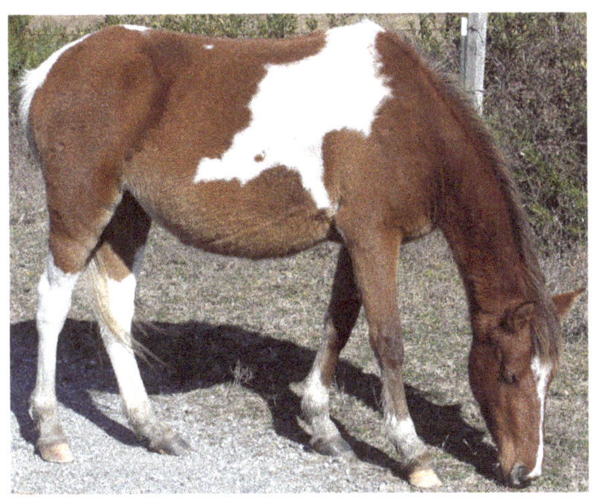

Bay Pinto

Doctor Amrien

Doc
mare
brand: 14

Doctor Amrien

Bay Pinto

White Saddle

mare
brand: 13

White Saddle

Bay Pinto

Miracle's Natural Beauty

mare
brand: 09

Bay Pinto

Miracle's Natural Beauty

Bay Pinto

May's Grand Slam

May
mare
brand: 12

Bay Pinto

May's Grand Slam

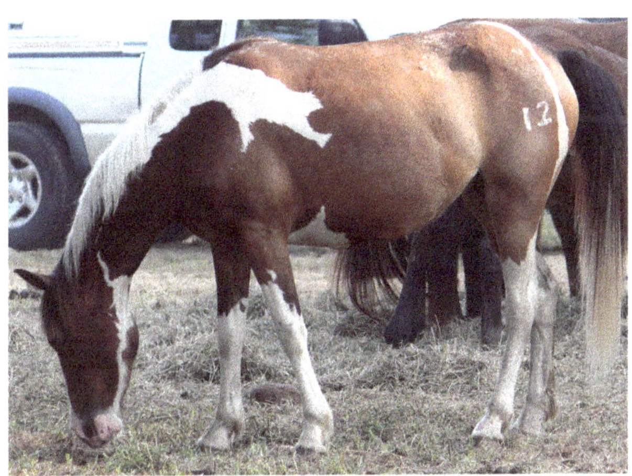

Bay Pinto

Carol's Little Freedom

Little Freedom
mare
brand: 99, partial

Bay Pinto

Carol's Little Freedom

Bay Pinto

Tunie

Queenie
mare
brand: 03

Bay Pinto

Tunie

Bay Pinto

Ajax

stallion
brand: 07, partial

Ajax

Bay Pinto

Babe

mare
brand: 94, partial

Bay Pinto

Babe

Bay Pinto

Rainbow Warrior

Napolean
stallion
brand: none

Bay Pinto

Rainbow Warrior

Bay Pinto

Destiny Feathering Spirit

Destiny
mare
brand: none

Bay Pinto

Destiny Feathering Spirit

Bay Pinto

Sweetheart

mare
brand: unreadable

Bay Pinto

Sweetheart

Bay Pinto

Splash

Danny's Girl
mare
brand: 14

Splash

Bay Pinto

Grandma's Dream

mare
brand: 13

Bay Pinto

Grandma's Dream

Bay Pinto

Loveland's Secret Feather

Secret, Feather
mare
brand: 12

Bay Pinto

Loveland's Secret Feather

Bay Pinto

Wild Thing

stallion
brand: none

Bay Pinto

Wild Thing

Bay Pinto

Chickadee

mare
brand: 13

Chickadee

Bay Pinto

Wildest Dreams

mare
brand: 08

Bay Pinto

Wildest Dreams

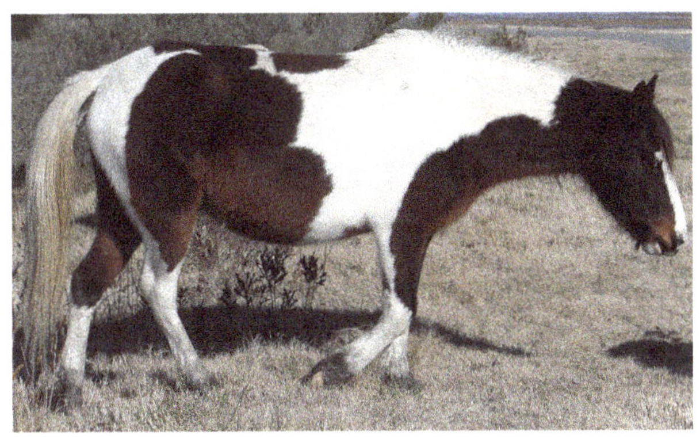

Bay Pinto

Black Star

mare
brand: none

Bay Pinto

Black Star

Bay Pinto

Marguerite of Chincoteague

mare
brand: 13

Bay Pinto

Marguerite of Chincoteague

Bay Pinto

Shy Anne

Half n Half
mare
brand: none

Shy Anne

Bay Pinto

Dream Catcher

mare
brand: 97

Bay Pinto

Dream Catcher

Bay Pinto

Fifteen Friends of Freckles

Freckles
mare
brand: 06

Bay Pinto

Fifteen Friends of Freckles

Bay Pinto

Skylark

mare
brand: none

Skylark

Bay Pinto

Scotty ET

ET
mare
brand: 02, partial

Bay Pinto

Scotty ET

Bay Pinto

CLG Wild Star

Wild Star
mare
brand: 16

CLG Wild Star

Bay Pinto

Seaside Miracle

mare
brand: F

Seaside Miracle

Bay Pinto

A Splash of Freckles

Splash of Freckles
mare
brand: unreadable

Bay Pinto

A Splash of Freckles

Bay Pinto

Maverick

stallion
brand: 14

Maverick

Bay Pinto

Got Milk

Anna
mare
brand: none

Bay Pinto

Got Milk

Black

CLG Surfer's Blue Moon

Blue, Blue Moon, Surfer's Blue Moon
mare
brand: 15

CLG Surfer's Blue Moon

Black Pinto

Ace's Black Tie Affair

Ace
stallion
brand: 07

Ace's Black Tie Affair

Black Pinto

Poco's Starry Night

Starry Night, Cash
mare
brand: 12

Poco's Starry Night

Black Pinto

Destiny's Shadowing Moonbeam

Shadow
mare
brand: 15

Black Pinto

Destiny's Shadowing Moonbeam

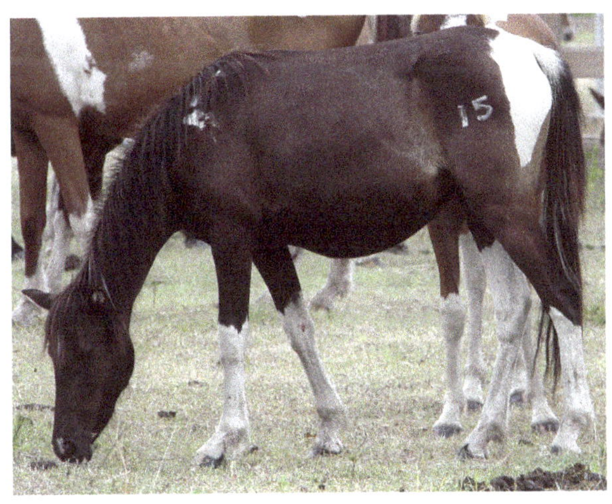

Black Pinto

Pixie Dust

mare
brand: 14

Pixie Dust

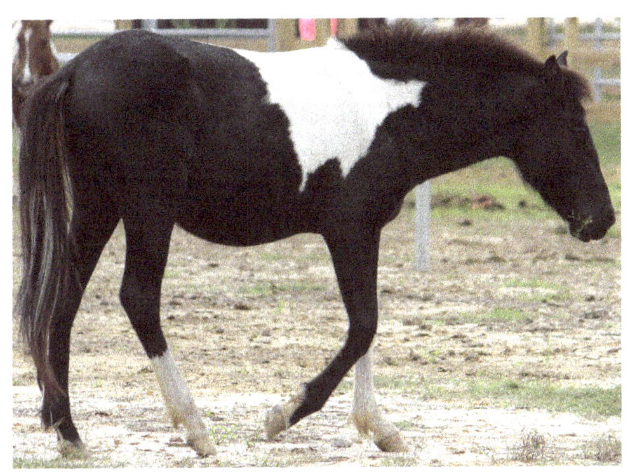

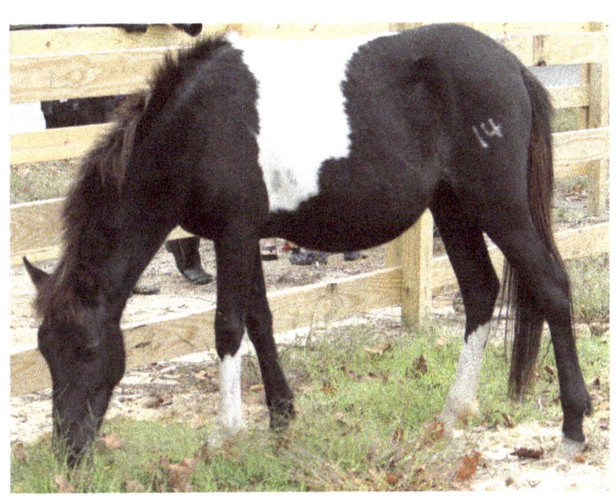

Black Pinto

Gracey

mare
brand: 13

Gracey

Black Pinto

Black Pearl

mare
brand: 14

Black Pearl

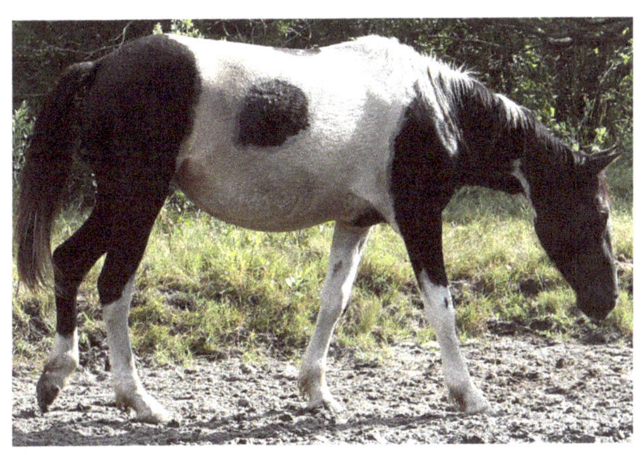

Black Pinto

Baybe

Baby
mare
brand: none

Baybe

Black Pinto

Beach Boy

Saltwater Renegade, Renegade
stallion
brand: 15

Beach Boy

Buckskin

Alice's Sandcastle

mare
brand: 12

Alice's Sandcastle

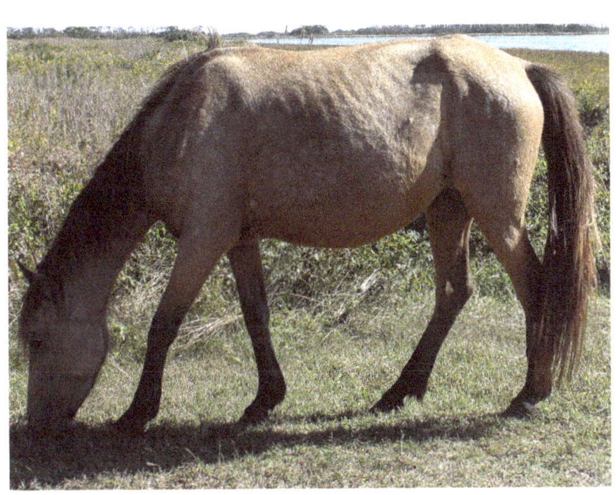

Buckskin

Ivana Marie Zustan

Zustan
mare
brand: 16

Ivana Marie Zustan

Buckskin

Jessica's Sea Star Sandy

Jessica's Sandy
mare
brand: 06

Jessica's Sea Star Sandy

Buckskin

Landrie's Georgia Peach

Georgia Peach
mare
brand: 04

Landrie's Georgia Peach

Buckskin

Poco Latte PW

mare
brand: 02

Poco Latte PW

Buckskin

Sunrise Ocean Tides

Sunny
mare
brand: 15

Sunrise Ocean Tides

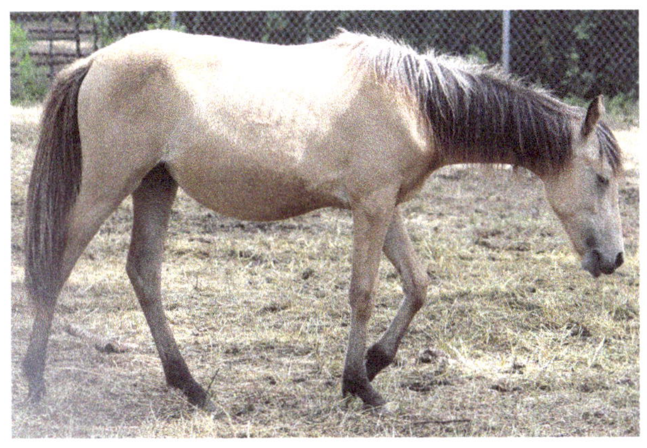

Buckskin

Too Grand

Salt Water Taffee
mare
brand: 00

Too Grand

Buckskin

Kachina Grand Star

Kachina
mare
brand: 05, partial

Kachina Grand Star

Buckskin Pinto

Molly's Rosebud

Rosie
mare
brand: none

Molly's Rosebud

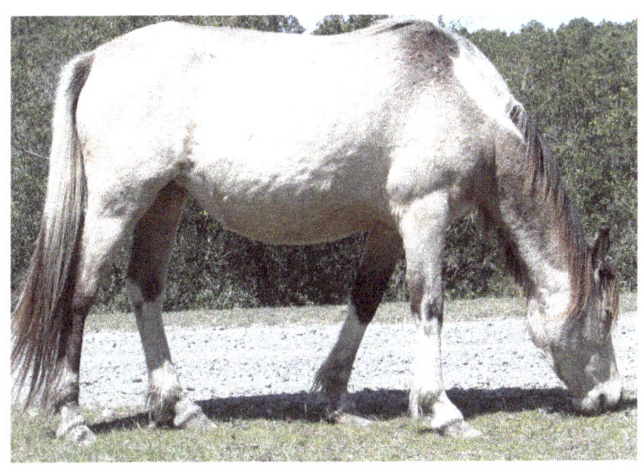

Buckskin Pinto

CLG Bay Princess

Bay Princess
mare
brand: 16

CLG Bay Princess

Buckskin Pinto

Badabing

mare
brand: 15

Badabing

Buckskin Pinto

Tornado's Legacy

Legacy, Lil Tornado
stallion
brand: 07

Tornado's Legacy

Buckskin Pinto

Randy

mare
brand: 14

Randy

Chestnut

Isle Treasure

La Flame
mare
brand: 94

Isle Treasure

Chestnut

JABATAA

mare
brand: 02

JABATAA

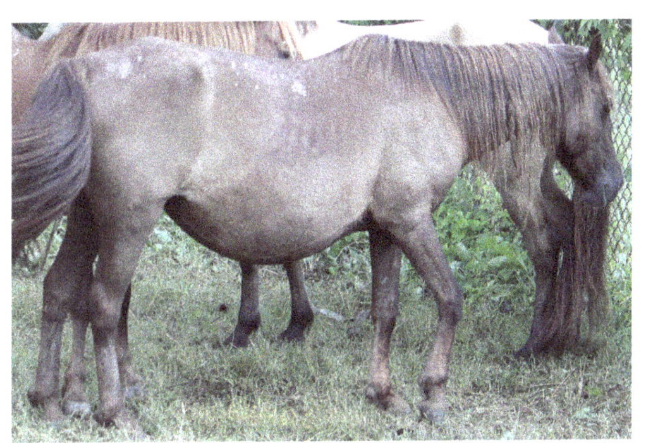

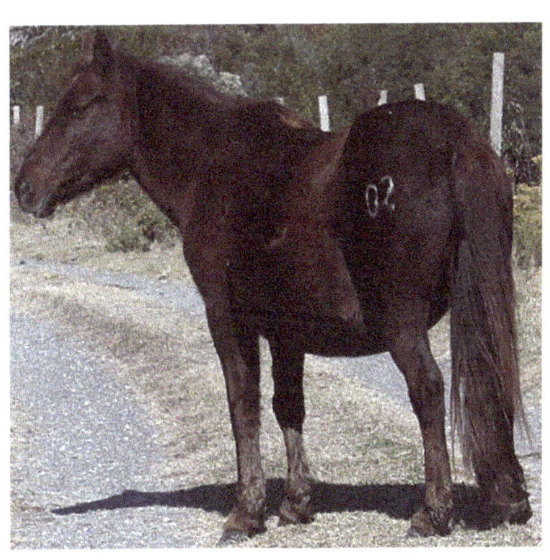

Chestnut

Surfer's Shining Star

Gingersnap
mare
brand: 15

Surfer's Shining Star

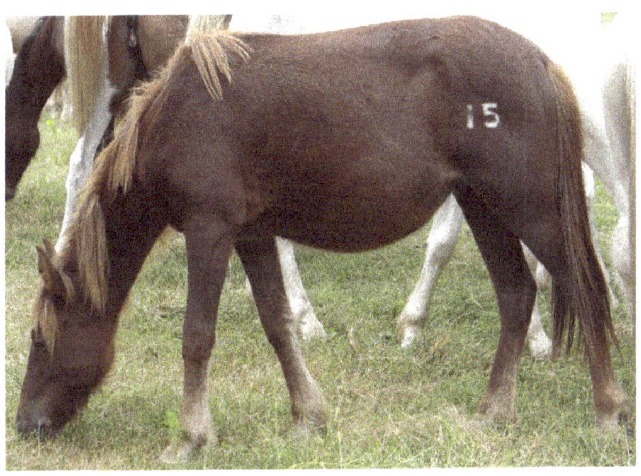

Chestnut

Surfin' Chantel

mare
brand: 13

Surfin' Chantel

Chestnut

Susana

mare
brand: 01

Susana

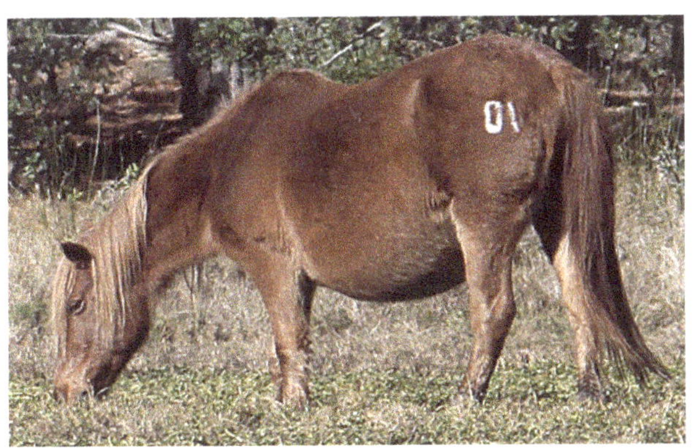

Chestnut

Suzy's Sweetheart

mare
brand: 98

Suzy's Sweetheart

Chestnut

TSG's Elusive Star

Elusive Star
mare
brand: 05, 5

TSG's Elusive Star

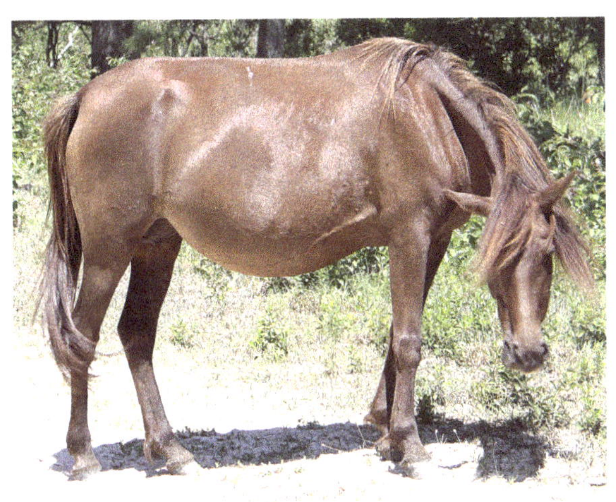

Chestnut

Wild Island Orchid

Naughty Lady
mare
brand: unreadable

Wild Island Orchid

Chestnut

Shashay Lady

mare
brand: 97

Shashay Lady

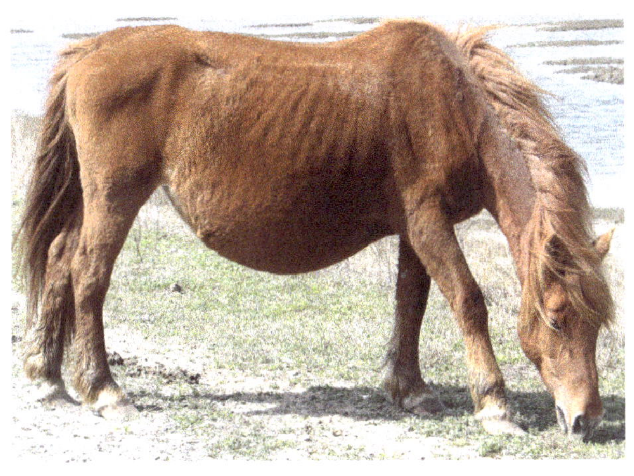

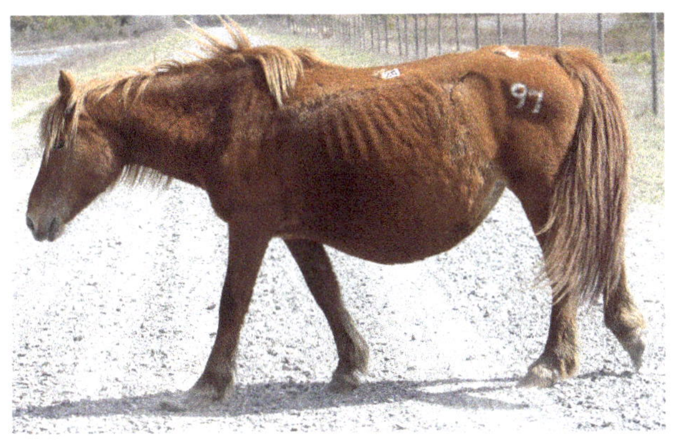

Chestnut

Tuleta Star

mare
brand: 02

Tuleta Star

Chestnut

Cinnamon Blaze

mare
brand: unreadable

Cinnamon Blaze

Chestnut

Kimmee-Sue

mare
brand: 12

Kimmee-Sue

Chestnut

Surfin' Scarlet

Scarlet
mare
brand: 00

Surfin' Scarlet

Chestnut

Precious Jewel

mare
brand: 14

Precious Jewel

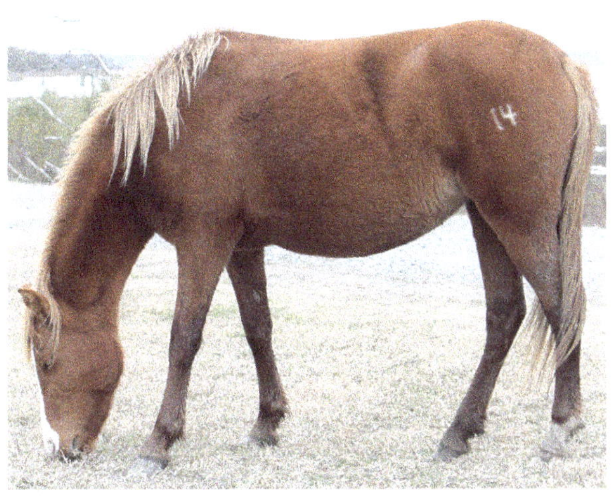

Chestnut

Surf Queen

Gone With The Wind
mare
brand: none

Surf Queen

Chestnut

Unforgettable 2001

Diamond
mare
brand: none

Unforgettable 2001

Chestnut

Judy's Little Smooch

Smooch
mare
brand: none

Judy's Little Smooch

Chestnut

Lyra's Vega

mare
brand: 05

Lyra's Vega

Chestnut

Surfer Princess

mare
brand: 15

Surfer Princess

Diamond's Jewel

Jewel
mare
brand: 06, partial

Diamond's Jewel

Chestnut

Phantom Mist

Fabio
stallion
brand: none

Phantom Mist

Chestnut Pinto

Catwalk's Olympic Glory

Glory
mare
brand: 16

Chestnut Pinto

Catwalk's Olympic Glory

Chestnut Pinto

Carol's Lightning Rose

Lightning, Courtney's Boy's Lightning
mare
brand: 16

Chestnut Pinto

Carol's Lightning Rose

Chestnut Pinto

America's Sweetheart

mare
brand: none

Chestnut Pinto

America's Sweetheart

Chestnut Pinto

Slash of White

mare
brand: 98

Slash of White

Chestnut Pinto

Lefty's Checkmark

Butterfly
mare
brand: none

Lefty's Checkmark

Chestnut Pinto

CJ SAMM'N

mare
brand: 06

CJ SAMM'N

Kimball's Rainbow Delight

Rainy, Rainbow Delight
mare
brand: 06, partial

Chestnut Pinto

Kimball's Rainbow Delight

Chestnut Pinto

Tiger Lily

Waterbaby
mare
brand: none

Tiger Lily

Chestnut Pinto

Susie Q

Lady Hook
mare
brand: 96

Susie Q

Chestnut Pinto

Catwalk Chaos

Margarita
mare
brand: none

Catwalk Chaos

Chestnut Pinto

Anne Bonny

mare
brand: none

Chestnut Pinto

Anne Bonny

Chestnut Pinto

TJ's Firefly

Firefly
mare
brand: 16

Chestnut Pinto

TJ's Firefly

Chestnut Pinto

Sweet Jane

Duckie
mare
brand: 06, partial

Chestnut Pinto

Sweet Jane

Chestnut Pinto

Little Duckie

Quackers
mare
brand: F

Little Duckie

Chestnut Pinto

Carnival Baby

Booku
mare
brand: 05

Carnival Baby

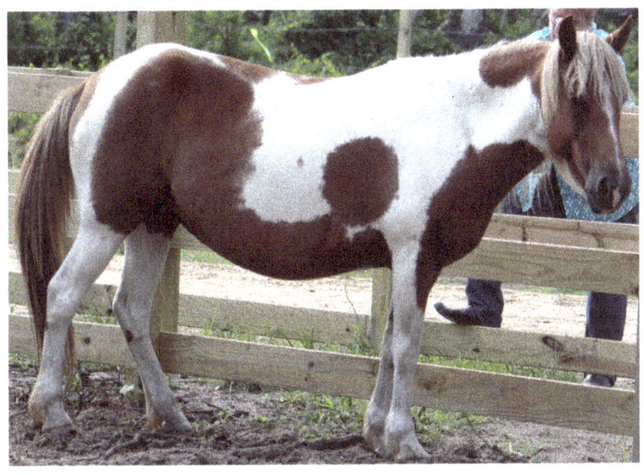

Chestnut Pinto

Misty Mills

mare
brand: 06, partial

Misty Mills

Chestnut Pinto

Beach Bunny

mare
brand: 15

Chestnut Pinto

Beach Bunny

Chestnut Pinto

Archer's Gambit

Puzzle, Little Frog
stallion
brand: 08

Chestnut Pinto

Archer's Gambit

Chestnut Pinto

Checkers

Giraffe
mare
brand: 7, partial

Checkers

Chestnut Pinto

Stevenson's Dakota Sky

Dakota, Dakota Sky
mare
brand: 01

Chestnut Pinto

Stevenson's Dakota Sky

Chestnut Pinto

Butterfly Kisses

mare
brand: 06

Chestnut Pinto

Butterfly Kisses

Chestnut Pinto

Courtney's Island Dove

Dove
mare
brand: unreadable

Chestnut Pinto

Courtney's Island Dove

Chestnut Pinto

Little Bit O' Joansie

mare
brand: 14

Little Bit O' Joansie

Chestnut Pinto

Don Leonard Stud II

Leonard Stud II
stallion
brand: 14

Chestnut Pinto

Don Leonard Stud II

Chestnut Pinto

Essie

mare
brand: 13

Essie

Chestnut Pinto

Thetis

mare
brand: 01

Chestnut Pinto

Thetis

Chestnut Pinto

Sonny's Legacy

mare
brand: 13

Sonny's Legacy

Chestnut Pinto

Dakota's Promise

mare
brand: 13

Chestnut Pinto

Dakota's Promise

Chestnut Pinto

Gidget's Beach Baby

Beach Baby
mare
brand: none

Gidget's Beach Baby

Chestnut Pinto

Witch Kraft

Friendly Girl
mare
brand: none

Witch Kraft

Chestnut Pinto

Thunderstorm Skies

Thunder
mare
brand: 13

Thunderstorm Skies

Palomino

Chief Golden Eagle

Chief
stallion
brand: 08

Chief Golden Eagle

Palomino

Kachina Mayli Mist

Mayli
mare
brand: 12

Kachina Mayli Mist

Palomino

Shy & Sassy Sweet Lady Suede

Suede
mare
brand: 14

Palomino

Shy & Sassy Sweet Lady Suede

Two Teague's Golden Girl

Goldie
mare
brand: 16

Two Teague's Golden Girl

Palomino Pinto

Calcetín

mare
brand: 13

Calcetín

Palomino Pinto

Tornado's Prince of Tides

Prince
stallion
brand: 07

Palomino Pinto

Tornado's Prince of Tides

Little Miss Sunshine

Sunshine
mare
brand: 15

Little Miss Sunshine

Palomino Pinto

Whisper of Living Legend

Whisper
mare
brand: 00

Palomino Pinto

Whisper of Living Legend

Palomino Pinto

Marina's Marsh Mallow

Marsh Mallow
mare
brand: 14

Palomino Pinto

Marina's Marsh Mallow

Palomino Pinto

Lorna Dune

mare
brand: 13

Lorna Dune

Silver Dilute

Surfer Dude's Gidget

Gidget
mare
brand: F, 02, partial

Surfer Dude's Gidget

Silver Dilute

Dreamer's Gift

mare
brand: 12

Dreamer's Gift

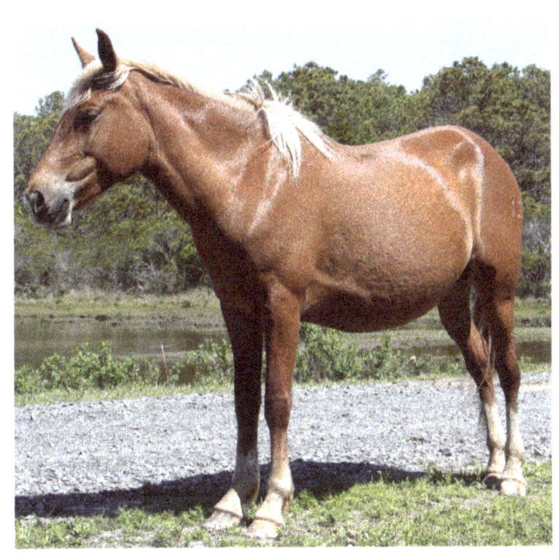

Ken

Valentine
stallion
brand: 08

Ken

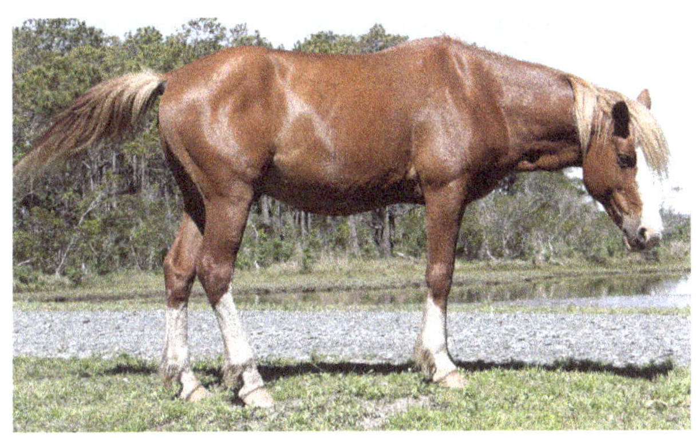

Silver Dilute

Surfer's Riptide

Riptide
stallion
brand: 09, partial

Surfer's Riptide

2017 Buy Backs

2017 Buy Backs

2017 Buy Backs

Alphabetical Index

A

A Splash of Freckles, bay pinto, 88
Ace *see* Ace's Black Tie Affair
Ace's Black Tie Affair, black pinto, 96
Ajax, bay pinto, 48
Alice's Sandcastle, buckskin, 112
America's Sweetheart, chestnut pinto, 184
Angel *see* Jean Bonde's Bayside Angel
Anna *see* Got Milk
Anne Bonny, chestnut pinto, 200
Archer's Gambit, chestnut pinto, 214

B

Babe, bay pinto, 50
Baby *see* Baybe
Badabing, buckskin pinto, 132
Bay Girl, bay, 2
Bay Princess *see* CLG Bay Princess
Baybe, black pinto, 108
Beach Baby *see* Gidget's Beach Baby
Beach Boy, black pinto, 110
Beach Bunny, chestnut pinto, 212
Black Pearl, black pinto, 106
Black Star, bay pinto, 70
Bling Bling, bay, 26
Blue *see* CLG Surfer's Blue Moon
Blue Moon *see* CLG Surfer's Blue Moon
Booku *see* Carnival Baby
Breezy *see* Summer Breeze
Butterfly *see* Lefty's Checkmark
Butterfly Kisses, chestnut pinto, 220

Alphabetical Index

C

Calcetín, palomino pinto, 250
Carnival Baby, chestnut pinto, 208
Carol's Lightning Rose, chestnut pinto, 182
Carol's Little Freedom, bay pinto, 44
Cash *see* Poco's Starry Night
Catwalk Chaos, chestnut pinto, 198
Catwalk's Olympic Glory, chestnut pinto, 180
Cee Cee *see* Summer Breeze
Checkers, chestnut pinto, 216
Chickadee, bay pinto, 66
Chief *see* Chief Golden Eagle
Chief Golden Eagle, palomino, 242
Cinnamon Blaze, chestnut, 158
CJ SAMM'N, chestnut pinto, 190
CLG Bay Princess, buckskin pinto, 130
CLG Surfer's Blue Moon, black, 94
CLG Wild Star, bay pinto, 84
Cody *see* Dakota Sky's Cody Two Socks
Cody's Little Jigsaw Puzzle, bay pinto, 34
Courtney's Boy's Lightning *see* Carol's Lightning Rose
Courtney's Island Dove, chestnut pinto, 222

D

Daisey, bay, 4
Dakota *see* Stevenson's Dakota Sky
Dakota Sky *see* Stevenson's Dakota Sky
Dakota Sky's Cody Two Socks, bay, 24
Dakota's Promise, chestnut pinto, 234
Danny's Girl *see* Splash
Destiny *see* Destiny Feathering Spirit

Destiny Feathering Spirit, bay pinto, 54
Destiny's Shadowing Moonbeam, black pinto, 100
Diamond *see* Unforgettable 2001
Diamond's Bay Dream *see* Bling Bling
Diamond's Jewel, chestnut, 176
Doc *see* Doctor Amrien
Doctor Amrien, bay pinto, 36
Don Leonard Stud II, chestnut pinto, 226
Dove *see* Courtney's Island Dove
Dream Catcher, bay pinto, 76
Dreamer's Gift, silver dilute, 264
Duckie *see* Sweet Jane

E

Effie's Papa Bear, bay, 6
Ella *see* Ella of Assateague
Ella of Assateague, bay pinto, 32
Elusive Star *see* TSG's Elusive Star
Essie, chestnut pinto, 228
ET *see* Scotty ET

F

Fabio *see* Phantom Mist
Feather *see* Loveland's Secret Feather
Fifteen Friends of Freckles, bay pinto, 78
Firefly *see* TJ's Firefly
Fluffy *see* Bay Girl
Freckles *see* Fifteen Friends of Freckles
Friendly Girl *see* Witch Kraft

G

Galadriel, bay, 8
Georgia Peach *see* Landrie's Georgia Peach

Gidget *see* Surfer Dude's Gidget
Gidget's Beach Baby, chestnut pinto, 236
Gingersnap *see* Surfer's Shining Star
Giraffe *see* Checkers
Glory *see* Catwalk's Olympic Glory
Goldie *see* Two Teague's Golden Girl
Gone With The Wind *see* Surf Queen
Got Milk, bay pinto, 92
Gracey, black pinto, 104
Grandma's Dream, bay pinto, 60

H

Half n Half *see* Shy Anne
Hoppy *see* Effie's Papa Bear

I

Isle Treasure, chestnut, 138
Ivana Marie Zustan, buckskin, 114

J

JABATAA, chestnut, 140
Jean Bonde's Bayside Angel, bay, 20
Jessica's Sandy *see* Jessica's Sea Star Sandy
Jessica's Sea Star Sandy, buckskin, 116
Jewel *see* Diamond's Jewel
Jigsaw *see* Cody's Little Jigsaw Puzzle
Judy's Little Smooch, chestnut, 170

K

Kachina *see* Kachina Grand Star
Kachina Grand Star, buckskin, 126
Kachina Mayli Mist, palomino, 244
Ken, silver dilute, 266
Kimball's Rainbow Delight, chestnut pinto, 192

Kimmee-Sue, chestnut, 160

L

La Flame *see* Isle Treasure
Lady *see* Pony Ladies' Sweet Surprise
Lady Hook *see* Susie Q
Landrie's Georgia Peach, buckskin, 118
Leah's Bayside Angel, bay, 22
Lefty's Checkmark, chestnut pinto, 188
Legacy *see* Tornado's Legacy
Leonard Stud II *see* Don Leonard Stud II
Lightning *see* Carol's Lightning Rose
Lil Tornado *see* Tornado's Legacy
Little Bit O' Joansie, chestnut pinto, 224
Little Dolphin, bay, 10
Little Duckie, chestnut pinto, 206
Little Freedom *see* Carol's Little Freedom
Little Frog *see* Archer's Gambit
Little Miss Sunshine, palomino pinto, 254
Lorna Dune, palomino pinto, 260
Loveland's Secret Feather, bay pinto, 62
Lyra's Vega, chestnut, 172

M

Margarita *see* Catwalk Chaos
Marguerite of Chincoteague, bay pinto, 72
Marina's Marsh Mallow, palomino pinto, 258
Marsh Mallow *see* Marina's Marsh Mallow
Maverick, bay pinto, 90
May *see* May's Grand Slam
May's Grand Slam, bay pinto, 42
Mayli *see* Kachina Mayli Mist

Miracle's Natural Beauty, bay pinto, 40
Misty Mills, chestnut pinto, 210
Molly's Rosebud, buckskin pinto, 128

N

Napolean *see* Rainbow Warrior
Naughty Lady *see* Wild Island Orchid
Neptune *see* Little Dolphin

P

Pappy's Pony, bay, 12
Phantom Mist, chestnut, 178
Pixie Dust, black pinto, 102
Poco Latte PW, buckskin, 120
Poco's Starry Night, black pinto, 98
Pony Ladies' Sweet Surprise, bay, 14
Poseidon's Fury *see* Effie's Papa Bear
Precious Jewel, chestnut, 164
Prince *see* Tornado's Prince of Tides
Puzzle *see* Archer's Gambit

Q

Quackers *see* Little Duckie
Queenie *see* Tunie

R

Rainbow Delight *see* Kimball's Rainbow Delight
Rainbow Warrior, bay pinto, 52
Rainy *see* Kimball's Rainbow Delight
Randy, buckskin pinto, 136
Renegade *see* Beach Boy
Riptide *see* Surfer's Riptide
Rosie *see* Molly's Rosebud
Rosie's Teapot, bay pinto, 28

S

Salt Water Taffee *see* Too Grand
Saltwater Renegade *see* Beach Boy
Scarlet *see* Surfin' Scarlet
Scotty ET, bay pinto, 82
Seaside Miracle, bay pinto, 86
Secret *see* Loveland's Secret Feather
Shadow *see* Destiny's Shadowing Moonbeam
Shashay Lady, chestnut, 154
Shy & Sassy Sweet Lady Suede, palomino, 246
Shy Anne, bay pinto, 74
Skylark, bay pinto, 80
Slash of White, chestnut pinto, 186
Smooch *see* Judy's Little Smooch
Sonny's Legacy, chestnut pinto, 232
Splash, bay pinto, 58
Splash of Freckles *see* A Splash of Freckles
Starry Night *see* Poco's Starry Night
Stevenson's Dakota Sky, chestnut pinto, 218
Suede *see* Shy & Sassy Sweet Lady Suede
Summer Breeze, bay pinto, 30
Sunny *see* Sunrise Ocean Tides
Sunrise Ocean Tides, buckskin, 122
Sunshine *see* Little Miss Sunshine
Surf Queen, chestnut, 166
Surfer Dude's Gidget, silver dilute, 262
Surfer Princess, chestnut, 174
Surfer's Blue Moon *see* CLG Surfer's Blue Moon
Surfer's Riptide, silver dilute, 268
Surfer's Shining Star, chestnut, 142
Surfin' Chantel, chestnut, 144

Surfin' Scarlet, chestnut, 162
Susana, chestnut, 146
Susie Q, chestnut pinto, 196
Suzy's Sweetheart, chestnut, 148
Sweet Jane, chestnut pinto, 204
Sweetheart, bay pinto, 56

T

Taco *see* Two Teagues Taco
Thetis, chestnut pinto, 230
Thunder *see* Thunderstorm Skies
Thunderstorm Skies, chestnut pinto, 240
Tiger Lily, chestnut pinto, 194
TJ's Firefly, chestnut pinto, 202
Too Grand, buckskin, 124
Tornado's Legacy, buckskin pinto, 134
Tornado's Prince of Tides, palomino pinto, 252
TSG's Elusive Star, chestnut, 150
Tuleta Star, chestnut, 156
Tunie, bay pinto, 46
Two Teague's Golden Girl, palomino, 248
Two Teagues Taco, bay, 16

U

Unci, bay, 18
Unforgettable 2001, chestnut, 168

V

Valentine *see* Ken

W

Waterbaby *see* Tiger Lily
Whisper *see* Whisper of Living Legend
Whisper of Living Legend, palomino pinto, 256

White Saddle, bay pinto, 38
Wild Island Orchid, chestnut, 152
Wild Star *see* CLG Wild Star
Wild Thing, bay pinto, 64
Wildest Dreams, bay pinto, 68
Witch Kraft, chestnut pinto, 238

Z

Zustan *see* Ivana Marie Zustan

Stallion Index

Bay

Effie's Papa Bear, 6
Little Dolphin, 10

Bay Pinto

Ajax, 48
Maverick, 90
Rainbow Warrior, 52
Wild Thing, 64

Black Pinto

Ace's Black Tie Affair, 96
Beach Boy, 110

Buckskin Pinto

Tornado's Legacy, 134

Chestnut

Phantom Mist, 178

Chestnut Pinto

Archer's Gambit, 214
Don Leonard Stud II, 226

Palomino

Chief Golden Eagle, 242

Palomino Pinto

Tornado's Prince of Tides, 252

Silver Dilute

Ken, 266
Surfer's Riptide, 268

Brand Index

00

Ella of Assateague, bay pinto, 32
Surfin' Scarlet, chestnut, 162
Too Grand, buckskin, 124
Whisper of Living Legend, palomino pinto, 256

01

Stevenson's Dakota Sky, chestnut pinto, 218
Susana, chestnut, 146
Thetis, chestnut pinto, 230

02

JABATAA, chestnut, 140
Poco Latte PW, buckskin, 120
Scotty ET, bay pinto, 82
Surfer Dude's Gidget, silver dilute, 262
Tuleta Star, chestnut, 156

03

Pappy's Pony, bay, 12
Tunie, bay pinto, 46

04

Landrie's Georgia Peach, buckskin, 118
Pony Ladies' Sweet Surprise, bay, 14

05

Carnival Baby, chestnut pinto, 208
Dakota Sky's Cody Two Socks, bay, 24
Kachina Grand Star, buckskin, 126
Lyra's Vega, chestnut, 172
TSG's Elusive Star, chestnut, 150
Two Teagues Taco, bay, 16

Brand Index

06

Butterfly Kisses, chestnut pinto, 220
CJ SAMM'N, chestnut pinto, 190
Diamond's Jewel, chestnut, 176
Fifteen Friends of Freckles, bay pinto, 78
Jessica's Sea Star Sandy, buckskin, 116
Kimball's Rainbow Delight, chestnut pinto, 192
Misty Mills, chestnut pinto, 210
Sweet Jane, chestnut pinto, 204

07

Ace's Black Tie Affair, black pinto, 96
Ajax, bay pinto, 48
Tornado's Legacy, buckskin pinto, 134
Tornado's Prince of Tides, palomino pinto, 252

08

Archer's Gambit, chestnut pinto, 214
Chief Golden Eagle, palomino, 242
Ken, silver dilute, 266
Little Dolphin, bay, 10
Wildest Dreams, bay pinto, 68

09

Miracle's Natural Beauty, bay pinto, 40
Surfer's Riptide, silver dilute, 268

12

Alice's Sandcastle, buckskin, 112
Dreamer's Gift, silver dilute, 264
Kachina Mayli Mist, palomino, 244
Kimmee-Sue, chestnut, 160
Loveland's Secret Feather, bay pinto, 62

May's Grand Slam, bay pinto, 42
Poco's Starry Night, black pinto, 98

13

Calcetín, palomino pinto, 250
Chickadee, bay pinto, 66
Cody's Little Jigsaw Puzzle, bay pinto, 34
Dakota's Promise, chestnut pinto, 234
Essie, chestnut pinto, 228
Gracey, black pinto, 104
Grandma's Dream, bay pinto, 60
Lorna Dune, palomino pinto, 260
Marguerite of Chincoteague, bay pinto, 72
Rosie's Teapot, bay pinto, 28
Sonny's Legacy, chestnut pinto, 232
Surfin' Chantel, chestnut, 144
Thunderstorm Skies, chestnut pinto, 240
White Saddle, bay pinto, 38

14

Black Pearl, black pinto, 106
Doctor Amrien, bay pinto, 36
Don Leonard Stud II, chestnut pinto, 226
Little Bit O' Joansie, chestnut pinto, 224
Marina's Marsh Mallow, palomino pinto, 258
Maverick, bay pinto, 90
Pixie Dust, black pinto, 102
Precious Jewel, chestnut, 164
Randy, buckskin pinto, 136
Shy & Sassy Sweet Lady Suede, palomino, 246
Splash, bay pinto, 58

Brand Index

15

Badabing, buckskin pinto, 132
Beach Boy, black pinto, 110
Beach Bunny, chestnut pinto, 212
Bling Bling, bay, 26
CLG Surfer's Blue Moon, black, 94
Destiny's Shadowing Moonbeam, black pinto, 100
Jean Bonde's Bayside Angel, bay, 20
Little Miss Sunshine, palomino pinto, 254
Sunrise Ocean Tides, buckskin, 122
Surfer Princess, chestnut, 174
Surfer's Shining Star, chestnut, 142

16

Carol's Lightning Rose, chestnut pinto, 182
Catwalk's Olympic Glory, chestnut pinto, 180
CLG Bay Princess, buckskin pinto, 130
CLG Wild Star, bay pinto, 84
Ivana Marie Zustan, buckskin, 114
TJ's Firefly, chestnut pinto, 202
Two Teague's Golden Girl, palomino, 248

5

TSG's Elusive Star, chestnut, 150

7

Checkers, chestnut pinto, 216

94

Babe, bay pinto, 50
Isle Treasure, chestnut, 138

96

Susie Q, chestnut pinto, 196

97

Dream Catcher, bay pinto, 76
Shashay Lady, chestnut, 154

98

Slash of White, chestnut pinto, 186
Suzy's Sweetheart, chestnut, 148

99

Carol's Little Freedom, bay pinto, 44

F

Little Duckie, chestnut pinto, 206
Seaside Miracle, bay pinto, 86
Surfer Dude's Gidget, silver dilute, 262

Other Identification Resources

Book

The Field Guide to the Chincoteague Wild Ponies by Kelly Lidard

Identification Cards

Chincoteague Pony Identification Cards Decks 1 & 2 by Lois Szymanski, photography by Linda Kantjas
Deck 3 by DSC Photography

Smart Phone App

Chincoteague Pony Names by Gina Aguilera

Websites

Chincoteague Pony Pedigree Database at
www.chincoteaguepedigrees.com
DSC Photography at
www.dscphoto.smugmug.com